Literacy
Activity Book

Year 2 Term 2

UNIVERSITY COLLEGE CHICHESTER LIBRARIES

AUTHOR:

FIDGE

WS 2165821 8

TITLE:

LITERACY

CLASS NO:

CR
428 FID

DATE:

1-01

SUBJECT:

CR

D0416552

Every effort has been made to trace copyright holders and to obtain their permission for the use of copyright material. The authors and publishers would gladly receive information enabling them to rectify any error or omission in subsequent editions.

Acknowledgements
The Giant's Accidents © Charles Thomson, from *Another First Poetry Book*, published by Oxford University Press

Mr Gumpy's Outing by John Burningham © John Burningham

When I Was One by A. A. Milne from the *Now We Are Six* collection © A. A. Milne, published by Ted Smart Publishers

Why do Dogs Chase Cars? from *South and North, East and West* edited text © 1992 Michael Rosen. Reproduced by permission of the publisher Walker Books Ltd., London

The Caterpillar by Marc Brown, from *Hand Rhymes* published by HarperCollins Publishers Ltd

First published 1998
Reprinted 1998, 1999

Letts Educational, Schools and Colleges Division,
9–15 Aldine Street, London W12 8AW
Tel: 020 8740 2270   Fax: 020 8740 2280

Text © Louis Fidge

Designed by Gecko Limited, Bicester, Oxon
Produced by Ken Vail Graphic Design, Cambridge
Colour reproduction by PDQ Repro Ltd, Bungay, Suffolk

Illustrations by Sarah Geeves, Simon Girling Associates (Elizabeth Sawyer, Piers Harper), David Lock, GCI (Tim Archbold), Sylvie Poggio Artists Agency (Sarah Warburton, Bethan Matthews), Archer Art (Ross), John Plumb and Karen Donnelly

All our rights reserved. No part of this publication may be reproduced, stored in a retrieval system, or transmitted, in any form or by any means, electronic, mechanical, photocopying, recording or otherwise, without prior permission of Letts Educational.

British Library Cataloguing-in-Publication Data
A CIP record for this book is available from the British Library

ISBN 1 84085 184 8

Printed in Great Britain by Ashford Colour Press

Letts Educational is the trading name of BPP [Letts Educational] Ltd

Introduction

The Year 2 Literacy Textbooks:

◆ support the teaching of the Literacy Hour
◆ help meet the majority of the objectives of the National Literacy Strategy Framework
◆ are divided into three books, each containing one term's work
◆ contain ten units per term, each equivalent to a week's work

◆ provide one Self Assessment unit each term to check on progress
◆ contain one Writing Focus unit each term to support compositional writing
◆ provide coverage of a wide range of writing, both fiction and non-fiction as identified in the National Literacy Strategy Framework.

Unit number →

Text for reading and discussion

Key teaching points

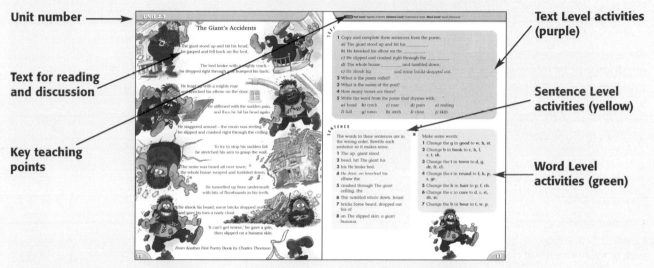

Text Level activities (purple)

Sentence Level activities (yellow)

Word Level activities (green)

Writing focus unit:

◆ appears on pages 26–27
◆ develops work covered in the preceding ten teaching units
◆ supports work on compositional writing
◆ contains support for the teaching of different essential writing skills.

The Glossary:

◆ contains and gives examples of key words and concepts
◆ contains illustrations to make meanings clearer where necessary
◆ may be used for teaching purposes or for reference by the pupil.

Self assessment unit:

◆ appears on pages 28–29
◆ reviews the key objectives at Sentence Level and Word Level in the preceding ten units
◆ contains a spelling chart to support the teaching of spelling strategies
◆ may be used to provide:
  – individual, group or class activities
  – a review of progress when completed and kept as a record
  – further practice in areas of concern
  – homework assignments.

High frequency word list:

◆ contains words that occur frequently in children's reading and writing
◆ helps children to recognise these words on sight and spell them correctly
◆ is often referred to and used in the activities in the book
◆ provides an easily accessible resource for spelling activities and a ready reference section.

Focus		
Text Level	**Sentence Level**	**Word Level**
• Characterisation and settings	Subject/verb agreement; past tenses	Phonemes and antonyms
• Reading a flowchart	Sentence structure	Compound words
• Aspects of poetry	Grammatical sense	Vowel phonemes
• Characters, themes and settings	Speech marks	Vowel phonemes
• Aspects of poetry	Commas in lists	Vowel phonemes; consonant digraphs
• Alphabetical order; dictionaries	Grammatical sense	Syllables
• Characters and settings	Verb tenses	Prefixes 'un' and 'dis'; opposites
• Reading a flowchart; themes	Constructing simple sentences	Vowel phonemes
• Character and setting	Speech marks	Vowel phonemes
• Aspects of rhymes	Agreement	Rhyming

Book 2, Term 2

Writing focus	*Writing a story, poem and character profile; Using a glossary; Making a flowchart*	

Self assessment	*Review of Word and Sentence Level skills covered in Units 2.1–2.10 plus Handy hints for spelling words*	

CONTENTS

Enough for Two?

The sun was like a burning ball of fire, high in the blue sky. The road was long and dusty. The only thing Anwar could think of was water. He was hot! Very hot! Then, just ahead, he saw a well. 'I expect it will be dry, like the others,' he said to himself.

As he got nearer he saw a skinny dog lying beside it. Anwar could see its bones it was so thin. 'Get out of my way,' Anwar said. He was desperate to get to the well. He picked up a stone and dropped it into the darkness of the well. For a second there was silence and then Plop!

'Water,' cried Anwar. The dog whined pitifully.

The problem was that there was no bucket or or rope so Anwar had to climb down inside the well. It was slow going, and he had to cling on by his fingers and toes. At last he reached the bottom. There it was – beautiful, cool water. He poured some over his head and drank great gulps of it, until he felt completely refreshed.

He was just about to make his way out of the well again when suddenly a picture of the poor old dog came into his mind. 'He is just as much in need of a drink as I was,' he thought. 'But how can I carry some water up for him?' Then an idea came into his head.

A few minutes later, when he reached the top of the well, the dog looked up. Anwar smiled. 'Here you are. You must be thirsty. This water is for you,' he said and held out his boot – full of water! The poor old dog's tail wagged and his eyes lit up as if to say, 'Thank you!'

A story from India

TEXT

1 What was the weather like?

2 What was the road like?

3 Why was Anwar glad to see the well?

4 Why did he tell the dog to get out of his way?

5 Why did he drop a stone down the well?

6 Why did Anwar have to climb into the well?

7 How did Anwar feel when he reached the bottom of the well?

8 Did Anwar drink the water slowly or quickly? How do you know?

9 How did Anwar get water for the dog?

10 Write and say what you think of Anwar.

SENTENCE

Copy these sentences. Choose the correct verbs to finish the sentences.

1 Anwar _____ (was/were) hot.

2 He _____ (see/saw) a dog near a well.

3 Anwar _____ (go/went) towards the well.

4 He _____ (drop/dropped) a stone into the well.

5 Anwar _____ (climbs/climbed) to the bottom of the well.

6 He _____ (drink/drank) a lot of water.

7 Anwar suddenly _____ (thinks/thought) of the poor dog.

8 He _____ (carry/carried) some water up in his boot for the dog.

9 'Here you _____ (is/are). Here _____ (is/are) some water for you,' Anwar said.

WORD

1 In the passage, find a word containing: *a)* ee *b)* ear *c)* each

2 In the passage, find a word containing: *a)* ay *b)* ai *c)* ake

3 In the passage, find a word containing: *a)* ike *b)* igh *c)* y (as in fly)

4 In the passage, find a word containing: *a)* oa *b)* one *c)* ow

5 In the passage, find a word containing: *a)* ue *b)* ew *c)* ool

6 Copy these words. Write the opposite for each.
Do it like this: wet – dry

a) big   *b)* long   *c)* hot   *d)* high   *e)* near   *f)* thin

g) dark   *h)* down   *i)* slow   *j)* full   *k)* old   *l)* bottom

The Story of Milk

1

A cow needs plenty of grass and water to help her make milk.

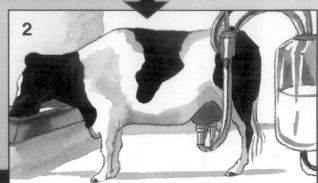

2

Every day the cow is milked. Milk is sucked from the cow by a machine.

3

Milk is collected from the farm in an insulated tanker to keep it cool.

4

The tanker takes the milk to the dairy.

5

At the dairy, milk is pasteurised to kill any germs. This means it is heated up and then cooled down quickly.

6

The pasteurised milk is put into plastic bottles or cartons ready to be sold.

TEXT

1 What does a cow need to help her make milk?

2 How often is a cow milked?

3 How is milk collected from the farm?

4 Where is the milk from the farm taken?

5 Why is milk pasteurised?

6 What happens to milk when it is pasteurised?

7 How do you know the order in which to read The Story of Milk?

8 What do you think happens after the milk has been put into bottles and cartons?

SENTENCE

1 Match up the beginnings and endings of these sentences. Write the complete sentences correctly.

a) Milk comes…   …from milk.

b) Cheese is made…   …is called a calf.

c) Supermarkets sell milk…   …from cows.

d) A baby cow…   …in plastic bottles or cartons.

2 Write a sensible ending for each of these sentences.

a) On farms you can ____ ____.   *b)* Every day _____.

c) Yoghurt is _____.   *d)* I enjoy _____.

e) Last night _____.   *f)* The ice cream was _____.

WORD

1 Do these word sums. Write the words you make.

a) farm + yard =   *b)* play + time =   *c)* sea + side =

d) bath + room =   *e)* sheep + dog =   *f)* key + hole =

2 Match up words from Set A with words from Set B to make longer words. Do it like this: run + way = runway

Set A	run after birth cloak foot fire mid snow
Set B	day way step night man noon room ball

The Giant's Accidents

The giant stood up and hit his head;
he gasped and fell back on the bed.

The bed broke with a mighty crack –
he dropped right through and bumped his back.

He leapt up with a mighty roar
and knocked his elbow on the door.

He stiffened with the sudden pain,
and then he hit his head again.

He staggered around – the room was reeling –
he slipped and crashed right through the ceiling.

To try to stop his sudden fall
he stretched his arm to grasp the wall.

The noise was heard all over town;
the whole house swayed and tumbled down.

He tunnelled up from underneath
with bits of floorboards in his teeth.

He shook his beard; some bricks dropped out
and gave his toes a nasty clout.

'It can't get worse,' he gave a grin,
then slipped on a banana skin.

From Another First Poetry Book *by Charles Thomson*

TEXT

1 Copy and complete these sentences from the poem.

a) The giant stood up and hit his _____.

b) He knocked his elbow on the _____.

c) He slipped and crashed right through the _____.

d) The whole house ___ _____ and tumbled down.

e) He shook his _____ and some bricks dropped out.

2 What is the poem called?

3 What is the name of the poet?

4 How many verses are there?

5 Write the word from the poem that rhymes with:

a) head   *b)* crack   *c)* roar   *d)* pain   *e)* reeling

f) fall   *g)* town   *h)* teeth   *i)* clout   *j)* skin

SENTENCE

The words in these sentences are in the wrong order. Rewrite each sentence so it makes sense.

1 The up. giant stood

2 head. hit The giant his

3 his He broke bed.

4 He door. on knocked his elbow the

5 crashed through The giant ceiling. the

6 The tumbled whole down. house

7 bricks Some beard. dropped out his of

8 on The slipped skin. a giant banana

WORD

Make some words:

1 Change the **g** in **good** to **w, h, st**.

2 Change **b** in **book** to **c, h, l, r, t, sh**.

3 Change the **t** in **town** to **d, g, dr, fr, cl**.

4 Change the **r** in **round** to **f, h, p, s, gr**.

5 Change the **h** in **hair** to **p, f, ch**.

6 Change the **c** in **care** to **d, r, st, sh, sc**.

7 Change the **b** in **bear** to **t, w, p**.

Mr Gumpy's Outing

One day Mr Gumpy went out in his boat.

'May we come with you?' said the children.

'Yes,' said Mr Gumpy, 'if you don't squabble.'

'Can I come along, Mr Gumpy?' said the rabbit.

'Yes, but don't hop about.'

'I'd like a ride,' said the cat.

'Very well,' said Mr Gumpy. 'But you're not to chase the rabbit.'

'Will you take me with you?' said the dog.

'Yes,' said Mr Gumpy, 'but don't tease the cat.'

'May I come please, Mr Gumpy?' said the pig.

'Very well, but don't muck about.'

'Have you a place for me?' said the sheep.

'Yes, but don't keep bleating.'

'Can we come too?' said the chickens.

'Yes, but don't flap,' said Mr Gumpy.

'Can you make room for me?' said the calf.

'Yes, if you don't trample about.'

'May I join you, Mr Gumpy?' said the goat.

'Very well, but don't kick.'

For a little while they all went along happily but then… the goat kicked… the calf trampled… the chickens flapped… the sheep bleated… the pig mucked about… the dog teased the cat… the cat chased the rabbit… the rabbit hopped… the children squabbled… the boat tipped… and into the water they fell.

Then Mr Gumpy and the goat and the calf and the chickens and the sheep and the pig and the dog and the cat and the rabbit and the children all swam to the bank and climbed out to dry in the hot sun.

'We'll walk home across the fields,' said Mr Gumpy. 'It's time for tea.'

From Mr Gumpy's Outing *by John Burningham*

TEXT

1 Make a list of the characters in the story.

2 Which character did you like best? Say why.

3 Where did the story take place?

4 What was the weather like? Say how you can tell.

5 Why do you think Mr Gumpy was in his boat?

6 Why did Mr Gumpy tell the animals not to mess about?

7 What is the story all about?

8 How does the story end?

SENTENCE

Copy these sentences. Write the things each character said inside the speech marks.

1 "_____?" said the children.

2 "_____?" said the rabbit.

3 "_____," said the cat.

4 "_____?" said the dog.

5 "_____?" said the pig.

6 "_____?" said the sheep.

7 "_____?" said the chickens.

8 "_____?" said the calf.

9 "_____?" said the goat.

WORD

1 Find a word in the story containing:

   a) ea   *b)* ee   *c)* oa   *d)* ay   *e)* ou   *f)* oi   *g)* oo

2 Think of other words containing each of the phonemes above.

3 Write and say what each animal did.
   Do it like this: The goat kicked.

Two Poems to Enjoy

When I Was One

When I was One,
I had just begun.

When I was Two,
I was nearly new.

When I was Three,
I was hardly Me.

When I was Four,
I was not much more.

When I was Five,
I was just alive.

But now I'm Six, I'm as clever as clever.
So I think I'll be six now for ever and ever.

From the Now We Are Six collection *by A. A. Milne*

What is Pink?

What is pink? A rose is pink
By the fountain's brink.
What is red? A poppy's red
In its barley bed.
What is blue? The sky is blue
Where the clouds float through.
What is white? A swan is white
Sailing in the light.
What is yellow? Pears are yellow,
Rich, and ripe, and mellow.
What is green? The grass is green,
With small flowers between.
What is violet? Clouds are violet
In the summer twilight.
What is orange?
Why, an orange is orange,
Just an orange!

By Christina Rossetti

TEXT

1 What is the title of the first poem?

2 Who wrote it?

3 How many verses does it have?

4 Find a word in the poem that rhymes with:

a) one *b)* two *c)* three
d) four *e)* five *f)* clever

5 Say something you liked about the poem.

6 What is the title of the second poem?

7 What is the name of the poet who wrote it?

8 How many questions are there in the poem?

9 Write what you think each of these words mean:

a) brink *b)* mellow *c)* twilight

10 Find and read some more poems by A. A. Milne and Christina Rossetti.

SENTENCE

1 Copy these lists and put in the missing commas.

Do it like this: pink, red, blue and yellow

a) green blue white and pink

b) cat dog mouse and hamster

c) book comic letter and magazine

d) apple orange pear and banana

e) plate cup dish and saucer

f) hammer saw screw and nail

g) tea coffee water and cola

h) pencil pen crayon and felt-tip

2 Write some more lists. Set them out like the ones above.

Write a list of four:

a) vegetables

b) wild animals

c) farm animals

d) insects

e) flowers

f) trees

WORD

1 Find words in the poems which contain:

a) ai *b)* ight *c)* ite *d)* ue *e)* ar *f)* ew *g)* ough

2 Think of another word containing each of the phonemes above.

3 Copy these words. Fill in the gaps with either 'wh' or 'ph'.

a) _ _ ere *b)* _ _ en *c)* ele _ _ ant *d)* _ _ oto

e) _ _ o *f)* gra _ _ *g)* _ _ y *h)* _ _ ich

An Animal Dictionary

Here is the start of an animal dictionary I am making.

	alligator	An alligator is a large reptile that lives in rivers and swamps in America and China.
	bear	A bear is a very big, heavy, wild animal with thick fur.
	camel	A camel comes from countries with hot deserts. They can go for a long time without eating.
	deer	A deer is an animal that eats grass. Some deers have antlers. Deer can run fast.
	elephant	The elephant is the largest land animal. It has a trunk and two tusks. It lives in Africa and India.
	fox	A fox looks like a dog with a long bushy tail. It lives in the wild.
	giraffe	A giraffe is a tall animal with a very long neck and long legs. It comes from Africa.
	hedgehog	A hedgehog is a small animal with prickles on its back.

TEXT

1 Write the name of the animals in the dictionary beginning with 'a', 'd' and 'g'.

2 Think of other animals beginning with each letter, from 'a' to 'h'.

3 What would the next five letters of the dictionary be?

4 'The animals in the dictionary are in alphabetical order.'
Explain what this means.

5 Here is a definition of one animal. 'It is a very big, heavy, wild animal with thick fur.' Which animal is this?

6 Copy the definition of a camel from the dictionary.

7 Use a dictionary. Look up and copy the definition for:

   a) an ant   *b)* a badger   *c)* a cheetah   *d)* a dog   *e)* an emu

SENTENCE

The animals in these sentences have got mixed up.

Write each sentence correctly so it makes sense.

1 A **dog** has whiskers and purrs.

2 A **cat** likes bones and barks.

3 A **sheep** squeaks and has a long tail.

4 A **fox** lives in a stable and eats hay.

5 A **bird** gives us wool and eats grass.

6 A **horse** clucks and lays eggs.

7 A **mouse** has wings and flies.

8 A **chicken** is like a wild dog and hunts at night.

WORD

Say these words and listen carefully:

bear is made of one syllable

hedge/hog is made of two syllables

el/e/phant is made of three syllables

bat	**hen**	**badger**
snake	**crocodile**	**monkey**
fox	**tiger**	**ostrich**
mouse	**kangaroo**	**horse**

1 Which of the words in the box are made of one syllable?

2 Which of the words are made of two syllables?

3 Which of the words are made of three syllables?

4 Think of two more animals which have one syllable.

5 Think of two more animals which have two syllables.

Why Do Dogs Chase Cars?

Some time ago, when cars first came to the roads, a donkey, a goat and a dog took a ride in a taxi to the villages where they lived.

When they reached the first village, the donkey tapped the driver on the shoulder. 'This is where I'm getting out, driver,' he said. 'How much?'

'Three thousand francs,' said the driver.

The donkey paid up and on went the goat and dog in the taxi. Soon the goat asked to be dropped off.

'How much?' he asked.

'Three thousand francs,' said the driver.

The goat jumped from the taxi and scampered off into the bush.

At long last the dog got to where he wanted to go.

'How much?' said the dog.

'Three thousand francs,' said the driver.

The dog held up a five thousand franc note. The driver grabbed the note, and drove off down the road, roaring with laughter.

Donkeys stay right where they are. They let the driver go round them. They know they paid up. They've done nothing wrong so they've got nothing to be ashamed of.

The moment a car comes down the road and there's a goat around, it'll scamper off as fast as it can because it knows that it didn't pay the fare and the driver is looking for his money.

Dogs spend their whole time chasing cars, looking for the driver who once cheated them.

So now you know why animals all do different things when a car comes down the road.

A traditional story from Northern Ghana from
South and North and East and West, ed. Michael Rosen

TEXT

1   What is the title of the story?

2   Where does the story come from?

3   Who or what are the four main characters in the story?

4   Which animal paid the taxi driver the correct money?

5   Which animal got out without paying?

6   Which animal gave the driver a five thousand franc note?

7   Was the taxi driver an honest man?

8   How does a donkey behave when a car comes down the road?

9   Why do dogs chase cars?

10   Do you think the story is true? Explain your answer.

SENTENCE

Copy these sentences. Choose the correct word from the brackets.

1 A car _____ (comed/came) down the road.

2 The donkey, goat and dog _____ (saw/seed) a taxi.

3 The animals _____ (taked/took) a ride in a taxi.

4 They _____ (went/goed) to a village.

5 "Let me out here," _____ (sayed/said) the donkey.

6 The goat _____ (asked/askt) to be dropped off.

7 The taxi driver _____ (drived/drove) off down the road.

8 The dog _____ (held/holded) up his money.

WORD

1 Choose 'un' or 'dis' to go in front of each word to make the opposite.
Do it like this: lucky – unlucky

a) lucky   *b)* safe   *c)* agree   *d)* well   *e)* fair

f) trust   *g)* pack   *h)* honest   *i)* load   *j)* like

2 Now write the words you made in two sets – 'un' words and 'dis' words.

3 Choose two words from each set. Make up some sentences and include the
words you have chosen.

The Caterpillar

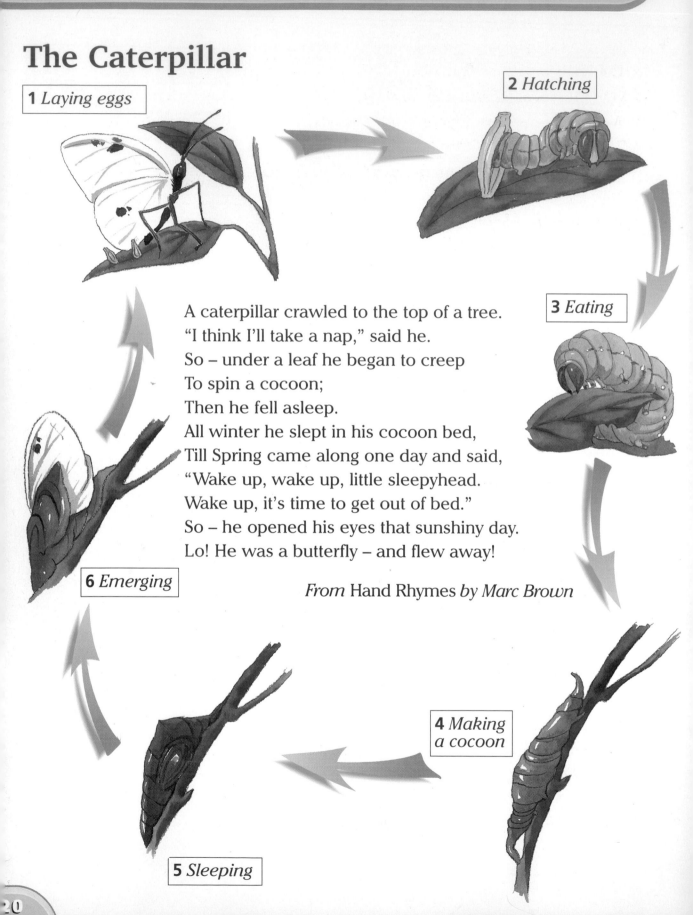

1 *Laying eggs*

2 *Hatching*

3 *Eating*

A caterpillar crawled to the top of a tree.
"I think I'll take a nap," said he.
So – under a leaf he began to creep
To spin a cocoon;
Then he fell asleep.
All winter he slept in his cocoon bed,
Till Spring came along one day and said,
"Wake up, wake up, little sleepyhead.
Wake up, it's time to get out of bed."
So – he opened his eyes that sunshiny day.
Lo! He was a butterfly – and flew away!

From Hand Rhymes *by Marc Brown*

6 *Emerging*

4 *Making a cocoon*

5 *Sleeping*

TEXT

1 The pictures tell a story. What is it?

2 What happens after the butterfly lays its eggs?

3 What does a caterpillar eat?

4 What does a caterpillar make to sleep in?

5 What happens to the caterpillar while it is inside the cocoon?

6 What is the poem about?

7 Write something you liked about the poem.

8 How do the pictures help you understand the poem better?

SENTENCE

Write a simple sentence about each picture. The first is done for you.

1 A butterfly lays its eggs on flowers or leaves.

When you have finished, read your sentences to make sure they make sense.

WORD

bird	fur	term	church	girl	butter
hurt	stir	shirt	person	burn	winter

1 Copy this chart. Write the words from the box in the correct columns.

'ir' words	'ur' words	'er' words
bird	fur	

2 Copy these sentences. Choose words from the box above to fill the gaps.

a) A bear has a lot of _____.

b) The _____ flew into the trees.

c) I fell over and tore my _____.

d) I spread some _____ on my bread.

e) It is very cold in the _____.

f) I heard the _____ bells ringing.

Ma Liang and the Magic Brush

Once upon a time there was a boy who liked drawing but he was too poor to buy a brush. One night he said to himself, 'If only I had a brush, I could draw pictures for the poor people in my village.'

Suddenly an old man with a long white beard appeared. 'Don't be frightened,' he said. 'Here's a brush for you. But you must only draw pictures for poor people with it.'

Ma Liang began to draw a hen, and as he did so it changed into a real hen. 'Wow!' he said. 'This brush must be magic!'

Then he saw a poor woman cutting wood. 'You need an axe,' he said. So he drew an axe and it changed into a real one.

Next he saw a poor farmer pulling a plough. 'You need a buffalo to pull your plough,' Ma Liang said. So he drew a buffalo and it changed into a real buffalo.

'Thank you. You are very kind,' the farmer said to Ma Liang.

Soon the king heard about Ma Liang's magic brush. 'Draw me a tree with gold coins hanging on it,' he ordered.

'You have plenty of gold. You don't need any more,' Ma Liang replied. The king was angry. 'Throw him in prison!' he cried. His soldiers caught hold of Ma Liang, threw him in prison and locked the door.

'If I had a key I could unlock the door,' Ma Liang said. So he drew a key and it changed into a real key. He opened the door quietly and escaped. When the king discovered that Ma Liang had got away, he got on his horse and chased him with his soldiers.

Ma Liang said, 'I need a horse.' So he drew one and it changed into a real horse. He jumped on it and galloped away.

A traditional story from China

TEXT

1 Who is the main character in the story?

2 Where does the story take place?

3 Who gave Ma Liang a paint brush?

4 What is special about the brush?

5 Which people did Ma Liang use the brush to help? How?

6 Was the king greedy or kind? Why?

7 In what way was Ma Liang clever when the king put him in prison?

8 How did Ma Liang use his paint brush to help him when he was being chased?

SENTENCE

Copy and complete these sentences.

1 "If only I had a brush," said _____.

2 "Here's a brush for you," said _____.

3 "This brush must be magic!" said _____.

4 "Thank you. You are very kind," said _____.

5 "Draw me a tree with gold coins hanging on it," ordered _____.

6 "You have plenty of gold. You don't need any more," said _____.

7 "Throw him in prison!" cried _____.

8 "If I had a key I could unlock the door," said _____.

WORD

1 Find a word in the passage containing each of these phonemes:

  a) or   *b)* oor   *c)* aw

  d) ore   *e)* au

2 Change the **f** in **fort** to s, **sh**, **p**, **sp**.

3 Change the **p** on **poor** to d, **fl**.

4 Change the **s** in **saw** to j, l, p, r, **cl**, **dr**, **str**.

5 Change the **m** in **more** to c, s, w, b, **st**.

6 Copy these words and fill in the gaps with 'au'.

  a) c _ _ ght   *b)* t _ _ ght

  c) d _ _ ghter   *d)* s _ _ cer

  e) p _ _ se   *f)* n _ _ ghty

  g) h _ _ l   *h)* _ _ thor

Rhymes Around the World

Susie Susie

Susie Susie suck your toe,
All the way to Mexico.
When you get there, cut your hair,
And don't forget your underwear.

A traditional poem from the USA

Hickety, bickety, pease, scone

Hickety, bickety, pease, scone,
Where shall this poor Scotsman gang?
Will he gang east, or will he gang west,
Or will he gang to the crow's nest?

A traditional poem from Scotland

Ting-a-ling-bone

Ting-a-ling-bone! Ting-a-ling-bone!
A fire broke out in the little goat's home.
A bucketful of water was fetched by the hen,
To put the fire out if she could, and then

The dogs from the farmhouse came as well,
They were bringing a ladder and ringing a bell.

Ting-a-ling-bone! Ting-a-ling-bone!
We'll put out the fire in the little goat's home.

A traditional poem from the Caribbean

Titli

Ek phool par bahti titli
Hans ka baccho se ye boli,
'Pankh dekh lo, nit aungi,
Tang kiya to urd jaungi.'

Butterfly sitting on a flower
Smiles to the children and says,
'I'll come every day. See my wings,
If you irritate me, I'll fly away.'

A traditional Hindi rhyme from India

TEXT

1 Where do the following rhymes come from?

a) Susie Susie   *b)* Hickety, bickety, pease, scone

c) Ting-a-ling-bone   *d)* Titli

2 Is Susie Susie a funny or sad rhyme?

3 *a)* Where is Susie going?   *b)* What must she do on her way there?

c) What must she do when she arrives?

4 What do you think 'gang' means in the Scottish poem?

5 *a)* In Ting-a-ling-bone, where was the fire?

b) Who fetched a bucketful of water?

c) What did the dogs bring?

6 *a)* Which two languages is Titli written in?

b) What do you think 'Ek phool par bahti titli' means?

7 Which was your favourite rhyme? Why?

SENTENCE

Copy these sentences. Correct the underlined words.

1 A butterfly <u>are</u> sitting on a flower.

2 Some children <u>is</u> playing.

3 Once upon a time there <u>were</u> a little girl.

4 The dogs <u>was</u> jumping up.

5 I <u>has</u> a television at home.

6 My television <u>have</u> five channels on it.

7 Last night I <u>done</u> my homework.

8 I <u>comes</u> from Scotland.

9 A dog <u>bark</u> but a cat purrs.

WORD

1 Find the pairs of rhyming words and write them down.

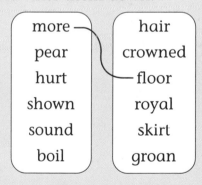

more	hair
pear	crowned
hurt	floor
shown	royal
sound	skirt
boil	groan

2 Think of a word that rhymes with each of the words below.

Do it like this: bird – heard

a) shirt   *b)* her   *c)* sport

d) claw   *e)* where   *f)* here

g) heart   *h)* sour   *i)* crowd

j) tune   *k)* note   *l)* why

25

1. Write a story

1 Read Unit 2.4 again. Imagine what happens next.

- ◆ All the animals go home with Mr Gumpy for tea.
- ◆ Where do they eat – in his house, in the garden?
- ◆ What does Mr Gumpy give each animal?
- ◆ Imagine that they all misbehave, just like in the boat.
- ◆ Write about the mess they make!

2 Imagine Mr Gumpy is in the jungle.

- ◆ He is rowing his boat down a river.
- ◆ Five different animals ask for a ride.
- ◆ What would he say to each of them?
- ◆ They all start misbehaving.
- ◆ What happens?
- ◆ Write about Mr Gumpy's Bad Day.

3 Read Unit 2.7 again.

- ◆ Make up a story about why dogs chase squirrels.

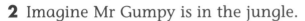

2. Write a poem

1 Read Unit 2.5 again.
Make up a poem about colours.
It doesn't have to rhyme.

Do it like this:

Red is the sun disappearing at the end of the day.

Blue is the warm sea and clear sky in the summer.

2 Make up a silly rhyme like Susie Susie in Unit 2.10.

3. Write a character profile

1 Read Unit 2.9 again. Here is a character profile of the king.

The king was a very rich man and very important, but he was not very kind. He lived in a castle and had lots of servants and soldiers. He wore expensive clothes and rode a white stallion. He had everything he wanted but he was a greedy man.

Draw a picture and write a character profile of Ma Liang.

4. Use a glossary

Use the glossary at the back of this book.

1 Write two things from it beginning with 'p'.

2 Write the definitions for a comma and for speech marks.

5. Make a flowchart

1 Here is a flow diagram of the life cycle of a frog. Write a sentence to go with each picture in your book.

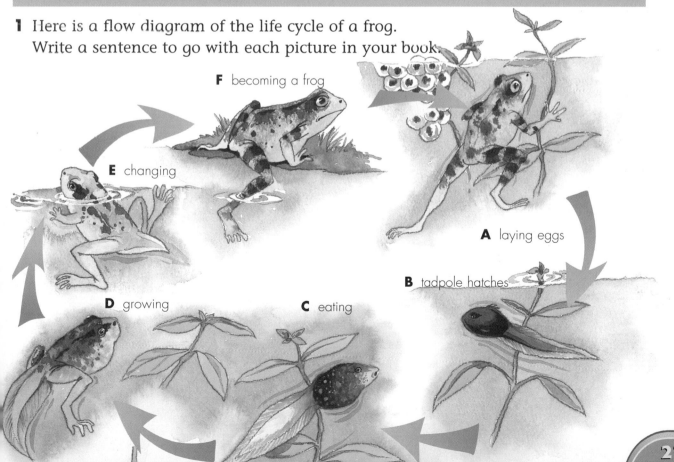

F becoming a frog

E changing

A laying eggs

D growing

C eating

B tadpole hatches

How are you getting on with the skills in the chart?
If you need extra practice, try the activities shown.

Grammar and punctuation	writing sensible sentences	1/2
	speech marks	3
	commas	4
Spelling, phonics and vocabulary	opposites	5
	compound words	6
	syllables	7
	consonant digraphs	8
	vowel phonemes	9/10

1 Match up the beginnings and endings of these
sentences and write them in your book.

a) We draw with…   …a knife.
b) We cut with…   …a spade.
c) We skip with…   …a pencil.
d) We dig with…   …a rope.

2 Copy these sentences. Correct the words that are underlined.

Yesterday Ben <u>go</u> to the seaside. He <u>takes</u> his swimming
trunks and <u>swimmed</u> in the sea. When he <u>get</u> out he <u>flied</u> his kite.

3 Copy the sentences and fill in what the children said.

Where are you going?

I'm going to the park.

May I come with you?

Yes you can.

Emma said, "_____?"

"_____," Ali replied.

"_____?" Emma asked.

Ali said, "_____."

4 Copy the list. Put in the missing commas: bread milk jam and tea.

5 Write the opposite of these words:

    a) fat   *b)* happy   *c)* hot   *d)* wet
    e) disappear *f)* unlucky   *g)* disagree *h)* dislike

6 Do these word sums. Write the words you make in your book.

    a) flag + pole =   *b)* bee + hive =
    c) bag + pipes =   *d)* bed + room =
    e) news + paper =   *f)* moon + light =

7 Copy these words. Write the number of syllables in each.

    Do it like this: mag/net (2)
    a) fish   *b)* comic
    c) pocket   *d)* cat
    e) lemonade *f)* caravan
    g) rabbit   *h)* difficult
    i) button   *j)* said

8 Copy these words. Choose 'wh' or 'ph' to fill in the gaps.

    a) _ _ at   *b)* _ _ one
    c) _ _ en   *d)* dol _ _ in
    e) _ _ ere   *f)* al _ _ abet
    g) ne _ _ ew   *h)* _ _ o

9 Look at page 28. Find a word containing:

    a) ee *b)* ai *c)* ay *d)* ow *e)* oo *f)* ou

10 Copy these words. Underline the two words with the same letter patterns in each set. The first one has been done for you.

    a) f<u>air</u> scare there p<u>air</u> bear
    b) tear care hair rare where
    c) door horn claw caught born
    d) more sport store taught draw

Handy hints for spelling words

Look – Look carefully at the word.

↓

Say – Say the word to hear how it sounds.

↓

Cover – Cover the word and try to see it in your mind.

↓

Write – Write the word from memory.

↓

Check – Check your spelling.

Glossary

alphabetical order

Words are often put in order according to the letter or order of letters they begin with. These words are in **alphabetical order**:

ant   **b**ear   **c**at   **d**og

character

Characters are the names of people, animals or things that appear in stories.

comma

A **comma** is a punctuation mark. It tells you to pause.

'My favourite colours are red, blue, green and yellow.'

compound word

A **compound word** is when two short words are joined to make one long word.

butter + fly = butterfly

consonant digraph

A **consonant digraph** is when two consonants come together and make one sound, like 'ch' or 'sh'.

fi**sh** and **ch**ips

definition

A **definition** is the meaning of a word.

dictionary

A **dictionary** gives you the meanings of words.

Dictionaries are arranged in alphabetical order.

flow diagram

A **flow diagram** is a sequence of pictures that explain how something is made or done.

glossary

A **glossary** is a list of special words and their meanings.

opposite

Opposites are two words whose meanings are as different as possible from each other.

hot   cold

phoneme

A **phoneme** is the smallest unit of sound in a word. It may be made up of one, two, three or four letters,

e.g. t**o**, sh**oe**, thr**ough**

poem

A **poem** is a piece of writing which is imaginative. It may express our thoughts or feelings. It is set out in lines. The lines may or may not rhyme.

prefix

A **prefix** is a group of letters that are added to the beginning of words to change their meaning.

happy   **un**happy

rhyme

A **rhyme** occurs when two words have an ending that sounds the same.

h**ead**   b**ed**

sentence

A **sentence** should make sense on its own. It should begin with a capital letter. Most sentences end with a full stop.

speech marks

When we write down what someone says, we put it inside **speech marks**.

The giant said, "I'm hungry."

syllable

Longer words may be broken down into smaller parts called **syllables**.

'bad' has one syllable

'bad/min/ton' has three syllables

title

A **title** is the name we give a book or something we have made.

verb

A **verb** is a doing word,

e.g. A dog **barks**.

verse

A poem is often divided into parts, or **verses**.

High frequency word list

about
after
again
an
another
as

back
ball
be
because
bed
been
boy
brother
but
by

call(ed)
came
can't
could

did
do
don't
door
down

first
from

girl
good
got

had
half
has
have
help
her
here
him

his
home
house
how

if

jump
just

last
laugh
little
live(d)
love

made
make
man
many
may
more
much
must

name
new
next
night
not
now

off
old
once
one
or
our
out
over

people
pull
push

put
ran

saw
school
seen
should
sister
so
some

take
than
that
their
them
then
there
these
three
time
too
took
tree
two

us

very

want
water
way
were
what
when
where
who
will
with
would

your

Days of the week:
Monday
Tuesday
Wednesday
Thursday
Friday
Saturday
Sunday

Months:
January
February
March
April
May
June
July
August
September
October
November
December

Colours:
black
blue
brown
green
pink
orange
purple
red
white
yellow

Numbers to twenty:
one
two
three
four
five
six
seven
eight
nine
ten
eleven
twelve
thirteen
fourteen
fifteen
sixteen
seventeen
eighteen
nineteen
twenty